HOW TO CREATE A POLLINATOR GARDEN

The Complete Guide to Planting, Maintaining Your
Own Pollinator Paradise

Graham F. Gardener

A Heartfelt Thank You

To all who have journeyed with us on the path of pollinator conservation, we extend our deepest gratitude and heartfelt thanks.

Thank you for taking the time to learn more about this important topic, for opening your hearts and minds to the wonders of the natural world, and for embracing the call to action to protect and preserve pollinators and the habitats they depend on.

Your curiosity, compassion, and commitment are beacons of light in a world that can sometimes feel dark and uncertain. Your willingness to listen, learn, and take action inspires us all to strive for a better, more sustainable future for ourselves and for generations to come.

Thank you for joining us on this journey of discovery, connection, and collective action. May your hearts be filled with gratitude for the beauty and abundance of the natural world, and may your actions be guided by a deep sense of love and reverence for all living things.

Together, we can make a difference. Together, we can protect pollinators and the precious ecosystems they inhabit. Together, we can create a world where flowers bloom, fruits ripen, and life flourishes in all its abundance and diversity.

With heartfelt thanks and deepest gratitude,

TABLE OF CONTENT

A Heartfelt Thank You 3

INTRODUCTION 7

Why Pollinator Gardens Are Important 9

Overview Of What Readers Will Learn In The Book .11

Chapter 1 Understanding Pollinators............................13

Explanation Of The Role Of Pollinators In Ecosystems
....13

Types Of Pollinators (Bees, Butterflies, Birds, Etc.) ..15

Their Habitat And Food Requirements 17

Chapter 2 Planning Your Pollinator Garden..................20

Assessing Your Space And Sunlight............................20

Choosing The Right Location 22

Design Considerations (e.g., Flower Colors, Plant
Heights, Blooming Seasons).......................................24

Chapter 3 Selecting Plants 27

Native vs. Non-Native Plants 27

Plant Species That Attract Different Pollinators 29

Creating A Diverse And Balanced Garden Ecosystem
....31

Chapter 4 Garden Maintenance 35

Soil Preparation And Fertilization 35

Watering Techniques 37

Pest And Weed Management Without Harmful Chemicals 40

Chapter 5 Attracting and Observing Pollinators 43

Providing Nesting Sites 43

Adding Water Sources 45

Tips For Observing And Identifying Pollinators In Your Garden 48

Chapter 6 Seasonal Care and Year-Round Interest 52

Planning For Continuous Bloom Throughout The Seasons 52

Winterizing Your Garden 54

Chapter 7 Troubleshooting Common Issues 58

Dealing With Pests And Diseases 58

Addressing Poor Pollinator Activity 61

Chapter 8 Community And Environmental Impact 65

Engaging With Local Organizations And Communities 65

Promoting Awareness & Education About Pollinator Conservation 68

15 Days Gardening Tracker 73

INTRODUCTION

In the heart of a bustling city, amidst the concrete jungle and urban sprawl, there lived a young woman named Tyla. With a heart as wild as the meadows she dreamt of, Tyla longed to bring a touch of nature's magic into her world—a world that seemed to pulse with life but lacked the gentle hum of pollinators and the vibrant colors of blooming flowers.

Tyla's journey began much like any other, with a seed of curiosity planted in her mind and a yearning for something more. She found herself drawn to the idea of creating a sanctuary for pollinators—a place where bees could dance among the blossoms and butterflies could flutter in the breeze. But as she stood in her tiny apartment, surrounded by concrete walls and city noise, she couldn't help but wonder: Where does one begin to create such a haven?

It was then that fate intervened, in the form scrolling online looking for Pollinator book then come across this book on a dusty shelf of a local bookstore. Its title, "How To Create a Pollinator Garden," beckoned to her with promises of secrets untold and dreams waiting to bloom. With trembling hands and a fluttering heart, Tyla cradled the book in her arms, knowing instinctively that it held the key to her wildest aspirations.

As she turned the pages, Tyla was transported into a world of possibility—a world where gardens bloomed with abandon and every flower whispered secrets of the earth. With each chapter, she discovered practical wisdom and heartfelt encouragement, guiding her through the intricacies of soil and sunlight, plant selection and garden design.

But it was not merely the knowledge contained within the pages that enchanted Tyla—it was the sense of connection, of belonging to something greater than herself. In the words of this author, she found a kindred spirit—a fellow wanderer on the path to pollinator paradise.

Armed with newfound confidence and a sense of purpose, Tyla set to work, transforming her humble balcony into a haven for pollinators. She watched with joy as bees buzzed and butterflies danced, their delicate wings brushing against petals painted with the colors of dawn.

And as she stood amidst the blossoms, with the scent of lavender in the air and the sun warming her face, Tyla knew that she had found her calling. She had become a steward of the earth, a guardian of the garden—a testament to the power of one person's dreams to change the world.

Dear reader, Tyla's journey is just the beginning—a testament to the transformative power of nature and the boundless potential within each of us. In "How To Create a Pollinator Garden," you'll find not only a guide to creating your own slice of paradise but also a companion on your journey—a friend to inspire, uplift, and guide you every step of the way.

So, let us embark together on this odyssey of discovery, where every page holds the promise of a brighter, more beautiful world. For in the garden of our dreams, anything is possible—and the seeds of change are waiting to be sown.

Why Pollinator Gardens Are Important

Close your eyes for a moment and imagine a world without flowers—without the vibrant hues of tulips, the delicate petals of roses, or the intoxicating scent of jasmine carried on the breeze. It's a world devoid of color, of scent, of life itself. Now, imagine a world without pollinators—a world where the buzz of bees and the flutter of butterflies are but distant memories, where fruits and flowers wither on the vine, unpollinated and unloved.

It's a world that none of us would want to inhabit, yet it's a reality that we face if we continue to neglect the plight of pollinators. For these humble creatures—bees, butterflies, birds, and bats—are not merely visitors in our gardens; they are the architects of life itself, the silent stewards of our ecosystems.

Pollinators are nature's matchmakers, facilitating the union between plant and pollen with a grace and efficiency that humbles the most skilled gardener. As they flit from flower to flower, they carry with them the promise of new life, ensuring the continuation of countless plant species and the abundance of fruits and vegetables that sustain us.

But the story of pollinators is not just one of ecological significance; it's a love story—a tale of symbiosis and interconnectedness that spans millennia. For as much as we depend on pollinators for our survival, they too rely on us for their well-being. In a world dominated by concrete and steel, our gardens serve as oases of refuge, offering sustenance and sanctuary to these tireless workers of the earth.

And so, dear reader, the importance of pollinator gardens cannot be overstated. They are not merely patches of green amidst a sea of gray; they are sanctuaries of life, beacons of hope in a world grown dim with indifference. They remind us of our kinship with nature, of our shared responsibility to nurture and protect the fragile web of life that sustains us all.

So, as you embark on your journey to create a pollinator garden, remember this: you are not just planting flowers; you are sowing the seeds of a brighter, more beautiful world. You are tending to the heartbeats of the earth, nurturing life in all its wondrous forms. And in doing so, you become part of a story—a story of love, of stewardship, and of the unbreakable bond between humanity and nature.

Overview Of What Readers Will Learn In The Book

Imagine stepping into a sun-dappled garden, where every flower holds a secret and every breeze whispers tales of wonder. This is the world we invite you to explore within the pages of "The Pollinator's Haven"—a world of possibility, creativity, and boundless beauty.

In this enchanting book, you'll embark on a journey unlike any other, guided by the gentle wisdom of those who have walked this path before you. Here's a glimpse of what awaits you:

Discovering the Secret Language of Pollinators: Delve into the fascinating world of bees, butterflies, and other pollinators, as we unravel the mysteries of their lives and the vital role they play in our ecosystems.

Designing Your Dream Garden: Learn the art of garden design, from choosing the perfect location to creating a harmonious landscape that delights the senses and nourishes the soul.

Selecting Plants with Purpose: Explore a treasure trove of plants, carefully curated to attract and sustain pollinators throughout the seasons. From native wildflowers to exotic blooms, you'll find inspiration for every corner of your garden.

Cultivating a Thriving Ecosystem: Master the art of garden care, with practical tips on soil preparation, watering techniques, and natural pest management. Cultivate a vibrant ecosystem where life flourishes and every creature finds its place.

Embracing the Joys of Observation: Open your eyes to the wonders of the natural world as we guide you through the art of pollinator observation. Learn to identify different species, understand their behaviors, and forge a deeper connection with the creatures that call your garden home.

Cultivating Community and Connection: Join a community of like-minded gardeners and conservationists as we explore the power of collective action in protecting pollinators and preserving biodiversity.

Nurturing a Legacy of Love: Plant the seeds of change for future generations as we celebrate the enduring legacy of pollinator gardens and the profound impact they have on our world.

Dear reader, within the pages of "The Pollinator's Haven," you'll find not just a guidebook, but a companion on your journey—a friend to inspire, uplift, and empower you as you embark on this odyssey of discovery. So come, let us wander together through fields of golden sunshine and fragrant blossoms, as we create a haven of beauty, harmony, and hope.

Chapter 1 Understanding Pollinators

Explanation Of The Role Of Pollinators In Ecosystems

Close your eyes and imagine a world without flowers—a world where fields lie barren, fruits refuse to ripen, and forests echo with silence. It's a world devoid of color, of scent, of life itself. Now, open your eyes and behold the miracle of pollinators—the humble heroes whose tireless efforts sustain the very fabric of our existence.

Pollinators, from bees and butterflies to birds and bats, are the unsung architects of life, the silent stewards of our ecosystems. Their delicate wings carry them from flower to flower, bearing with them the promise of new life as they facilitate the union between pollen and stigma.

But their role extends far beyond the mere act of pollination; they are the heartbeat of nature, the pulse that sustains life in all its wondrous forms. Without pollinators, many plant species would cease to exist, leading to a cascade of consequences that reverberate throughout the food chain.

Consider, for a moment, the humble bee—a creature so small, yet so mighty in its impact. As it flits from bloom to bloom, it not only ensures the reproduction of countless plant species but also provides a vital service to farmers and gardeners alike. From apples to almonds, cucumbers to cocoa, pollinators play a crucial role in the production of many of the foods we rely on for sustenance.

But their significance transcends mere utility; pollinators are symbols of resilience, adaptability, and interconnectedness. They remind us of the delicate balance of nature, of the intricate web of relationships that bind us all together in a tapestry of life.

And yet, despite their importance, pollinators face myriad threats—from habitat loss and pesticide use to climate change and disease. Their populations are dwindling, their habitats shrinking, their very existence hanging in the balance.

But there is hope, dear reader. In the gardens we tend, the flowers we plant, and the choices we make, we hold the power to protect and preserve these precious creatures. For in doing so, we not only safeguard the biodiversity of our planet but also ensure a future where flow`   ers continue to bloom, fruits continue to ripen, and life continues to flourish.

So let us stand together, hand in hand, as stewards of the earth and guardians of the garden. Let us honor the vital role of pollinators and pledge to do our part in nurturing a world where they can thrive, flourish, and continue to inspire wonder for generations to come.

Types Of Pollinators (Bees, Butterflies, Birds, Etc.)

Step into the enchanting world of pollinators, where a symphony of wings and colors awaits. From the industrious buzz of bees to the delicate flutter of butterflies, each creature plays a unique role in the intricate dance of pollination. Here are some of nature's most beloved pollinators:

Bees: Ah, the bees—nature's busiest workers and perhaps the most iconic of all pollinators. With their fuzzy bodies and buzzing wings, bees flit from flower to flower, collecting nectar and pollen to feed their colonies. From honeybees to bumblebees to solitary bees, these industrious insects are responsible for pollinating a staggering variety of plants, making them indispensable to ecosystems worldwide.

Butterflies: With their graceful wings and vibrant colors, butterflies are the epitome of beauty in motion. These delicate creatures sip nectar from flowers using their long, slender proboscis, inadvertently transferring pollen as they feed. While not as efficient as bees, butterflies play a crucial role in pollination, particularly for flowers with deep, tubular blossoms.

Birds: Take to the skies and behold the avian pollinators—nature's aerial acrobats and masters of flight. From hummingbirds to sunbirds to honeyeaters, these feathered wonders visit flowers in search of sweet nectar, their long bills and tongues perfectly adapted to reach deep within blossoms. As they sip nectar, they inadvertently collect and distribute pollen, ensuring the continued survival of many flowering plants.

Bats: As the sun sets and darkness falls, another group of pollinators emerges from the shadows—the bats. These nocturnal creatures play a vital role in pollinating night-blooming flowers, using their keen senses of smell and echolocation to locate their floral treasures. From deserts to rainforests, bats are essential pollinators in many ecosystems, ensuring the survival of plants that rely on their nocturnal visits.

Other Insects: Beyond bees and butterflies, a myriad of other insects contribute to the pollination process. From beetles to flies to ants, these unsung heroes visit flowers in search of food, inadvertently transferring pollen as they go about their daily lives. While they may not be as well-known as bees and butterflies, these insects are no less important in ensuring the reproduction of many plant species.

Together, these pollinators form a diverse and vibrant tapestry of life—a testament to the beauty and complexity of the natural world. Each creature, with its own unique traits and behaviors, plays a crucial role in the continuation of countless plant species, ensuring the continued abundance and diversity of life on our planet.

Their Habitat And Food Requirements

Picture a world where every flower holds the promise of sustenance—a world where pollinators find refuge and nourishment amidst the blooms. This is the habitat we strive to create for our winged friends, where their needs are met and their hearts are full.

Bee Abodes: Bees, those tireless workers of the garden, seek out habitats rich in nectar and pollen. From meadows teeming with wildflowers to urban gardens bursting with blooms, bees thrive in diverse landscapes where food sources abound. Some bees, like bumblebees, nest underground in abandoned rodent burrows or beneath leaf litter, while others, like solitary bees, seek shelter in hollow stems, wood crevices, or purpose-built bee hotels.

Butterfly Havens: Butterflies, with their delicate wings and ephemeral beauty, are drawn to habitats filled with sunshine and flowers. They prefer open spaces with ample sunlight and a variety of nectar-rich blooms to fuel their flights. Meadows, gardens, and forest clearings are popular haunts for butterflies, offering a buffet of blossoms to satisfy their hunger and support their delicate life cycle.

Avian Sanctuaries: Birds, those aerial acrobats of the skies, require habitats that provide both food and shelter. Hummingbirds, with their insatiable appetites for nectar, are often found in gardens filled with tubular flowers and dense foliage for nesting. Other avian pollinators, like sunbirds and honeyeaters, seek out a diverse array of flowering plants, from tropical rainforests to arid deserts, in search of sweet nectar and protein-rich insects.

Bat Dens: Bats, the silent guardians of the night, inhabit a variety of habitats, from caves and caverns to forests and deserts. They are drawn to areas with abundant flowering plants, particularly those that bloom at night or produce copious amounts of nectar. Tropical rainforests are hotspots for bat pollinators, providing a wealth of resources for these nocturnal creatures to thrive.

Insect Hideaways: Other insect pollinators, from beetles to flies to ants, make their homes in a myriad of habitats, each uniquely suited to their needs. Some prefer lush forests with a profusion of flowers, while others thrive in more urban environments, finding sustenance in gardens, parks, and green spaces.

In nurturing the habitats of pollinators, we not only provide for their physical needs but also foster a deeper connection with the natural world. For in creating spaces where flowers bloom and creatures thrive, we become stewards of the earth, guardians of the garden, and champions of life in all its wondrous forms.

Chapter 2 Planning Your Pollinator Garden

Assessing Your Space And Sunlight

Close your eyes and feel the warmth of the sun on your face, the gentle caress of a breeze as it whispers through the leaves. This is the canvas upon which your pollinator garden will bloom—a space filled with light, life, and endless possibilities.

Embracing the Light: Step outside and take a moment to observe the sunlight as it dances across your landscape. Notice the patterns of light and shadow, the way the sun moves throughout the day. Your pollinator garden will thrive in areas that receive ample sunlight, ideally at least six hours of direct sunlight per day. Look for open spaces, free from obstructions like tall buildings or dense tree canopies, where sunlight can reach your plants and nourish them from dawn till dusk.

Assessing Your Space: Take stock of your surroundings, from the size and shape of your garden to the layout of existing features like trees, shrubs, and structures. Consider how these elements will impact the amount of sunlight your garden receives and the types of plants you can grow. Is your space small and intimate, perfect for a container garden on a balcony or patio? Or is it expansive and open, beckoning you to create a sprawling meadow filled with wildflowers and native grasses? Whatever the size and shape of your space, there's a pollinator garden waiting to bloom.

Finding Balance: Strike a balance between sunlight and shade, creating microclimates within your garden that cater to a variety of plants and pollinators. In areas with intense sunlight, consider planting taller species or providing shade with trellises or pergolas. In shadier spots, opt for plants that thrive in low light conditions, like ferns or hostas. By embracing the nuances of light and shade, you'll create a dynamic and diverse garden that delights the senses and nurtures life in all its forms.

Listening to Nature's Call: As you assess your space and sunlight, listen to the whispers of nature guiding you on your journey. Pay attention to the needs of the land, the rhythms of the seasons, and the songs of the birds as they flit from branch to branch. Your garden is not just a place to grow plants; it's a living, breathing ecosystem—a sanctuary for pollinators and a reflection of your connection to the earth.

With each step you take, each ray of sunlight that illuminates your path, you're one step closer to creating your own pollinator paradise—a space where flowers bloom, bees buzz, and butterflies dance in the breeze. So open your heart to the light, embrace the beauty of your surroundings, and let nature be your guide as you embark on this odyssey of discovery.

Choosing The Right Location

Close your eyes and envision your ideal garden—a place where the earth sings with life, where flowers bloom with abandon, and where pollinators dance in the sunlight. This is the sanctuary you seek, the canvas upon which your dreams will take root and flourish.

Listening to Nature's Whispers: Step outside and listen to the whispers of the wind, the rustle of leaves, the chirping of birds. Nature has a language all its own, and it's speaking to you, guiding you towards the perfect location for your pollinator garden. Notice where the sunlight falls, where the soil feels rich and alive, where the air is filled with the scent of possibility. Trust your instincts, and let the land speak to you as you seek out the ideal spot to plant your seeds of intention.

Connecting with the Land: Take a moment to connect with the land beneath your feet, to feel its heartbeat pulsing with life. Whether you're working with a small plot of land or a sprawling landscape, every inch holds the potential for growth and transformation. Consider the lay of the land, the slope of the terrain, the drainage patterns—all of these factors will influence the health and vitality of your garden. Choose a location that feels harmonious with the natural contours of the land, where plants can thrive and pollinators can flourish.

Embracing Diversity: Look for a location that embraces diversity, both in terms of plant species and habitat types. A diverse garden is a resilient garden, capable of weathering the storms of change and supporting a wide array of pollinators throughout the seasons. Seek out spaces with a mix of sun and shade, open areas and sheltered nooks, where different plants and creatures can find their niche and coexist in harmony.

Considering Accessibility: Think about accessibility as you choose the location for your pollinator garden. Whether it's a backyard oasis, a community park, or a rooftop garden, make sure that your garden is easily accessible to you and others who wish to enjoy its beauty. Consider factors like proximity to water sources, ease of maintenance, and the presence of pathways or seating areas where visitors can linger and connect with nature.

Honoring the Spirit of Place: Above all, honor the spirit of place as you choose the location for your pollinator garden. Every landscape has its own unique story to tell, its own rhythm and flow that speak to the soul. By tuning in to the essence of the land, by listening to its whispers and heeding its call, you'll create a garden that is not just a reflection of your own desires, but a testament to the beauty and resilience of the natural world.

With each step you take, each moment of connection with the land, you're one step closer to creating a pollinator garden that is as unique and vibrant as you are. So trust in the wisdom of nature, follow your heart, and let the spirit of the land be your guide as you embark on this sacred journey of creation and discovery.

Design Considerations (e.g., Flower Colors, Plant Heights, Blooming Seasons)

Imagine standing amidst a sea of blossoms, each petal a brushstroke on nature's canvas, each flower a testament to the beauty of creation. This is the vision you hold in your heart as you embark on the journey of designing your pollinator garden—a journey of creativity, intention, and boundless possibility.

Choosing Your Palette: Think of your garden as a work of art, with flowers as your pigments and the earth as your canvas. Consider the colors that speak to your soul—the fiery oranges of marigolds, the serene blues of forget-me-nots, the cheerful yellows of sunflowers. Choose a palette that reflects your personality and complements the surrounding landscape, creating a tapestry of color that delights the senses and draws pollinators from far and wide.

Playing With Heights: Just as a painter uses light and shadow to create depth and dimension, so too can you play with heights in your garden to create visual interest and diversity. Think of your garden as a symphony of heights, with tall spires of delphiniums reaching towards the sky, mid-sized blooms like coneflowers and salvias dancing in the breeze, and low-growing groundcovers like creeping thyme carpeting the earth. By layering plants of different heights and textures, you'll create a garden that feels dynamic and alive, with something new to discover around every corner.

Dancing Through The Seasons: Like a melody that changes with the seasons, your garden should ebb and flow with the rhythms of nature, offering something new to discover with each passing month. Choose plants that bloom at different times of the year, from early spring bulbs like crocuses and daffodils to late summer perennials like asters and sedums. By embracing the full spectrum of the growing season, you'll ensure that your garden is alive with color and activity year-round, providing a constant source of nourishment and inspiration for pollinators and humans alike.

Creating Habitat: Beyond the flowers themselves, consider the broader habitat you're creating for pollinators in your garden. Provide shelter and nesting sites with features like rock piles, brush piles, and insect hotels. Include water sources like birdbaths or shallow dishes filled with pebbles for butterflies and bees to drink from. By attending to the holistic needs of pollinators, you'll create a garden that feels like a welcoming oasis—a place where creatures can rest, refuel, and thrive in harmony with the natural world.

Trusting Your Instincts: As you design your pollinator garden, trust in your instincts and let your heart be your guide. Listen to the whispers of nature, the gentle nudges of inspiration that guide your hand as you plant each seed and tend each bloom. Your garden is a reflection of your unique vision and creativity, a testament to the beauty and resilience of the human spirit. So trust in the process, embrace the journey, and let your garden be a celebration of life in all its infinite variety.

With each flower you plant, each design choice you make, you're weaving a tapestry of beauty and harmony—a garden that is as unique and vibrant as you are. So let your imagination soar, your heart sing, and your hands work their magic as you bring your pollinator paradise to life.

Chapter 3 Selecting Plants

Native vs. Non-Native Plants

Close your eyes and imagine a field alive with the colors of spring—a riotous tapestry of wildflowers dancing in the breeze. Now open your eyes and consider the plants you'll choose for your pollinator garden. Will you opt for the familiar blooms of non-native species, or will you heed the call of the wild and embrace the beauty of native plants?

The Case for Natives: There's a special magic in native plants—a connection to the land, a sense of belonging that resonates deep within the soul. Native plants have evolved alongside local pollinators over thousands of years, forming intricate relationships that are essential to the health and vitality of ecosystems. By choosing native species for your garden, you're not just creating a beautiful landscape; you're preserving a piece of your region's natural heritage, supporting biodiversity, and providing vital habitat for native pollinators.

Celebrating Diversity: Non-native plants, with their exotic blooms and foreign allure, certainly have their appeal. They add a splash of color and variety to the garden, expanding your palette and inviting you to explore new horizons. But while non-native plants may be beautiful, they often lack the resilience and adaptability of their native counterparts. They may require more water, fertilizer, and pesticides to thrive, posing a greater risk to the environment and the creatures that depend on it.

Striking a Balance: As you weigh the pros and cons of native vs. non-native plants, consider striking a balance that honors both the beauty of exotic blooms and the importance of native species. Incorporate a mix of plants from different regions and habitats, selecting non-invasive non-native species that complement rather than compete with native flora. By diversifying your garden and embracing a variety of plant species, you'll create a vibrant ecosystem that supports a wide array of pollinators and fosters resilience in the face of change.

Listening to the Land: Ultimately, the choice between native and non-native plants is a deeply personal one, rooted in your own values, experiences, and connection to the land. Listen to the whispers of nature as you select plants for your garden, paying attention to the needs of local pollinators and the rhythms of the seasons. Trust your instincts, follow your heart, and let the spirit of the land be your guide as you create a pollinator garden that is as unique and vibrant as you are.

With each plant you choose, each bloom that unfurls, you're making a statement—a statement of love for the earth, of reverence for the natural world, and of hope for the future. So plant with purpose, plant with passion, and let your garden be a testament to the beauty and resilience of native plants and the creatures that depend on them.

Plant Species That Attract Different Pollinators

Close your eyes and imagine a banquet spread before you—a feast for the senses, a symphony of colors and scents that dance on the breeze. Now open your eyes and behold the plants that will grace your pollinator garden, each one a tantalizing treat for the creatures that call it home.

Bee Buffet: Bees, those tireless workers of the garden, have discerning tastes when it comes to their dining preferences. They're drawn to flowers with bright colors and sweet nectar, like lavender, coneflowers, and bee balm. They also favor plants with flat, open blossoms that provide easy access to pollen and nectar, such as daisies, sunflowers, and asters. By planting a variety of bee-friendly flowers, you'll create a veritable smorgasbord that attracts bees of all shapes and sizes, from honeybees to bumblebees to solitary bees.

Butterfly Banquet: Butterflies, with their delicate wings and graceful flight, are partial to flowers with long, tubular blossoms that offer a convenient landing pad for their slender proboscis. They're particularly fond of brightly colored blooms with sweet nectar, like butterfly bush, milkweed, and butterfly weed. Butterflies also appreciate plants with broad, flat surfaces where they can bask in the sun and soak up the warmth, such as zinnias, lantanas, and verbena. By planting a mix of nectar-rich flowers that bloom throughout the season, you'll create a haven that attracts butterflies of all species and sizes, from monarchs to swallowtails to painted ladies.

Avian Feast: Birds, those aerial acrobats of the skies, have a taste for the exotic when it comes to their floral fare. They're drawn to flowers with bright colors and strong scents that stand out against the landscape, like trumpet vines, cardinal flowers, and honeysuckles. They also favor plants with tubular blossoms that are perfectly suited to their long, slender bills, such as salvia, penstemon, and fuchsia. By incorporating a mix of nectar-rich flowers and fruit-bearing shrubs, you'll create a banquet that attracts birds of all kinds, from hummingbirds to orioles to warblers.

Bat Buffet: Bats, those silent guardians of the night, have a taste for the exotic when it comes to their floral fare. They're drawn to flowers with pale, night-blooming blossoms that stand out against the darkness, like moonflowers, night-blooming jasmine, and evening primrose. They also favor plants with strong, musky scents that carry on the night air, such as yucca, agave, and cactus. By planting a mix of night-blooming flowers and fragrant shrubs, you'll create a feast that attracts bats of all species and sizes, from fruit bats to nectar bats to insect-eating bats.

Other Insect Invitations: Beyond bees, butterflies, birds, and bats, a myriad of other insects are drawn to the floral bounty of your garden. Beetles, flies, ants, and more all play a crucial role in pollination, and they each have their own unique preferences when it comes to their floral feasts. By planting a diverse array of flowers that appeal to a wide range of pollinators, you'll create a garden that teems with life and vitality, a sanctuary for creatures great and small.

With each plant you choose, each flower that blooms, you're extending an invitation—an invitation to the pollinators that will grace your garden with their presence, their beauty, and their vital role in the web of life. So plant with purpose, plant with passion, and let your garden be a testament to the interconnectedness of all living things.

Creating A Diverse And Balanced Garden Ecosystem

Close your eyes and envision a garden teeming with life—a symphony of colors, scents, and sounds that dance on the breeze. This is the vision you hold in your heart as you embark on the journey of creating a diverse and balanced ecosystem—a journey of stewardship, creativity, and connection.

Embracing Diversity: Just as a tapestry is woven from threads of many colors, so too is a garden enriched by the diversity of its inhabitants. Embrace diversity in all its forms, from the plants that grace your landscape to the creatures that call it home. Choose a wide variety of plant species, including natives and non-natives, annuals and perennials, to create a tapestry of color and texture that evolves with the seasons. Invite a menagerie of pollinators, from bees and butterflies to birds and bats, to partake in the banquet of nectar and pollen you've prepared. By embracing diversity in your garden, you'll create a rich and vibrant ecosystem that supports life in all its wondrous forms.

Fostering Balance: Like a conductor guiding an orchestra, strive to maintain balance and harmony in your garden ecosystem. Pay attention to the relationships between plants and pollinators, predators and prey, as you cultivate a space where all creatures can thrive. Encourage natural pest control by attracting beneficial insects like ladybugs, lacewings, and predatory wasps with companion planting and habitat features. Provide food, water, and shelter for wildlife throughout the year, ensuring that your garden is a welcoming oasis for creatures great and small. By fostering balance in your garden, you'll create a resilient and sustainable ecosystem that is in harmony with the natural world.

Nurturing Connections: Your garden is more than just a collection of plants; it's a living, breathing community—a web of connections that binds together plants, pollinators, and people in a tapestry of life. Nurture these connections by inviting others to share in the beauty and bounty of your garden, whether it's friends and family, neighbors and colleagues, or fellow gardeners and conservationists. Share stories and experiences, swap seeds and cuttings, and learn from one another as you cultivate a shared love for the earth and all its inhabitants. By nurturing connections in your garden, you'll create a sense of belonging and belongingness that extends far beyond its borders, fostering a deeper appreciation for the interconnectedness of all living things.

Tending with Care: Like a gardener tending to a delicate rose, tend to your garden with care and compassion, nurturing it with love and attention as it grows and evolves. Take the time to observe and listen, to notice the subtle changes that occur from day to day and season to season. Be mindful of the needs of your plants and pollinators, providing water during dry spells, shelter during storms, and protection from pests and diseases. Approach your garden with a spirit of curiosity and wonder, embracing the mysteries and marvels that unfold before you each day. By tending to your garden with care, you'll create a sanctuary of beauty and tranquility—a place where the soul can rest and the spirit can soar.

With each seed you sow, each flower that blooms, you're weaving a tapestry of life—a garden that is as diverse and balanced as it is beautiful. So tend to your garden with love and reverence, and let it be a reflection of the beauty and abundance of the natural world.

Chapter 4 Garden Maintenance

Soil Preparation And Fertilization

Close your eyes and imagine sinking your hands into the rich, dark earth—the smell of damp soil filling your senses, the promise of new life stirring beneath your fingertips. This is the beginning of your journey as a steward of the land, a caretaker of the earth, as you prepare the soil for your garden with love and reverence.

Getting Your Hands Dirty: Soil preparation begins with getting your hands dirty—digging, turning, and aerating the earth to create a welcoming environment for plants to take root and thrive. Take the time to remove any weeds, rocks, or debris from the soil, clearing the way for new growth to emerge. Break up compacted soil with a garden fork or tiller, loosening the earth and allowing air, water, and nutrients to penetrate deep into the soil profile. By tending to the physical needs of the soil, you'll lay the foundation for a healthy and productive garden.

Feeding the Earth: Like a chef preparing a nourishing meal, fertilization is the key to feeding the soil and providing essential nutrients for plant growth. Choose organic fertilizers that are gentle on the earth and free from harmful chemicals, such as compost, aged manure, or organic plant-based fertilizers. Spread a layer of compost or manure over the soil surface, then gently incorporate it into the top few inches of soil with a garden fork or rake. This will replenish the soil with organic matter, improve soil structure, and provide a steady supply of nutrients for your plants throughout the growing season.

Listening to the Land: As you prepare the soil and fertilize your garden, listen to the whispers of the land—the subtle cues and signals that guide your actions and inform your decisions. Pay attention to the texture and color of the soil, the presence of earthworms and other beneficial organisms, and the growth habits of nearby plants. These observations will help you gauge the health of your soil and determine its specific needs, whether it's adjusting the pH, increasing fertility, or improving drainage. By listening to the land and responding with care, you'll create a garden that is in harmony with the natural world and capable of supporting life in all its forms.

Cultivating Connection: Soil preparation and fertilization are not just tasks to be checked off a list; they're opportunities to cultivate a deeper connection with the earth and all its inhabitants. Approach these tasks with a sense of reverence and gratitude, acknowledging the gifts of the soil and the countless creatures that call it home. Take the time to slow down, to savor the sensation of soil between your fingers, the smell of earth after a summer rain. By cultivating connection with the land, you'll deepen your appreciation for the beauty and abundance of the natural world, and nurture a sense of stewardship that extends far beyond your garden's borders.

With each scoop of soil, each handful of compost, you're nurturing the earth and sowing the seeds of abundance—a garden that is not just a source of food and beauty, but a living, breathing ecosystem that sustains life in all its forms. So tend to your garden with love and care, and let it be a reflection of your deep connection with the earth and all its inhabitants.

Watering Techniques

Close your eyes and imagine the sound of rain falling softly on the leaves—the earth drinking deeply, the plants sighing in relief. This is the essence of watering your garden—a dance between you and the earth, a ritual of nourishment and renewal.

Timing is Everything: Like a well-timed symphony, watering your garden requires a delicate balance of timing and rhythm. When it's cooler outside and evaporation rates are lower, water your garden in the early morning or late evening. This allows the water to penetrate deep into the soil, reaching the roots where it's needed most, without the risk of excess moisture evaporating before it can be absorbed. By timing your watering sessions with care, you'll maximize the effectiveness of each drop and minimize water waste.

Gentle Soaking: Imagine standing beneath a gentle waterfall, feeling the water cascade over your skin, soothing and refreshing. This is the sensation you want to recreate as you water your garden—gentle, even, and thorough. Use a watering can, hose, or drip irrigation system to deliver water directly to the base of your plants, allowing it to soak deeply into the soil. Avoid spraying water directly onto the leaves, as this can promote fungal diseases and water loss through evaporation. Instead, focus on delivering water where it's needed most—at the roots—ensuring that your plants receive the hydration they crave without wasting a drop.

Mulching Magic: Picture a blanket of mulch spread beneath your feet, protecting the soil from the harsh rays of the sun, retaining moisture, and suppressing weeds. Mulching is a simple yet powerful technique that can help conserve water in your garden, reducing the need for frequent watering and promoting healthy soil moisture levels. Spread a layer of organic mulch, such as straw, wood chips, or shredded leaves, around the base of your plants, keeping it several inches thick to effectively retain moisture and suppress weeds. By mulching your garden beds, you'll create a microclimate that's cooler, moister, and more hospitable to plant roots, ensuring that your garden thrives even during the hottest, driest days of summer.

Listening to the Plants: As you water your garden, listen to the plants—their leaves rustling in the breeze, their roots reaching deep into the earth. Pay attention to the signals they're sending you—the drooping leaves, the wilting stems, the vibrant colors that speak of health and vitality. These cues will help you gauge the watering needs of your plants, allowing you to adjust your watering schedule and techniques accordingly. Trust in the wisdom of nature, and let the needs of your plants guide your actions as you nurture them with water and care.

Cultivating Connection: Watering your garden is not just a chore to be done—it's an opportunity to cultivate a deeper connection with the earth and all its inhabitants. Approach this task with a sense of reverence and gratitude, acknowledging the precious gift of water and the life-giving role it plays in sustaining life. Take the time to slow down, to savor the sensation of water flowing through your fingers, the sight of droplets glistening in the sunlight. By cultivating connection with water, you'll deepen your appreciation for its importance and nurture a sense of stewardship that extends far beyond your garden's borders.

With each drop of water, each moment of connection with the earth, you're nurturing the garden and fostering a deeper sense of harmony and balance in the world. So water your garden with love and care, and let it be a reflection of your deep connection with the earth and all its inhabitants.

Pest And Weed Management Without Harmful Chemicals

Close your eyes and imagine a garden buzzing with life—a symphony of colors, scents, and sounds that dance on the breeze. Now open your eyes and consider the pests and weeds that threaten to disrupt this harmony—the insects that munch on leaves, the weeds that choke out precious plants. How will you manage these challenges without resorting to harmful chemicals?

Cultivating Resilience: Just as a healthy immune system helps the body fend off illness, so too does a healthy garden have the resilience to withstand pest and weed pressures without the need for harmful chemicals. Start by building healthy soil rich in organic matter, which provides a strong foundation for plant growth and helps plants resist pests and diseases. Choose disease-resistant plant varieties and plant them in the right location with proper spacing and sunlight exposure. By cultivating resilience in your garden, you'll create an environment where plants can thrive and pests and weeds struggle to gain a foothold.

Integrated Pest Management: Imagine a delicate ecosystem where predators keep prey populations in check, where natural enemies maintain a delicate balance between pest and plant. This is the essence of integrated pest management (IPM)—a holistic approach that combines cultural, biological, and mechanical controls to manage pests without the use of harmful chemicals. Encourage beneficial insects like ladybugs, lacewings, and predatory wasps by planting nectar-rich flowers and providing habitat features like insect hotels and rock piles. Use physical barriers like row covers or hand-picking to manage pest populations when necessary. By integrating multiple strategies into your pest management plan, you'll create a dynamic and resilient ecosystem where pests are kept in check and beneficial insects thrive.

Weed Wisdom: Weeds are nature's opportunists—tenacious survivors that compete with garden plants for water, nutrients, and sunlight. Instead of reaching for the herbicide, consider embracing natural weed management techniques that work with nature, not against it. Mulching is one of the simplest and most effective ways to suppress weeds, smothering them beneath a blanket of organic material like straw, wood chips, or shredded leaves. Hand-pulling is another effective technique for removing weeds, especially when done regularly before they have a chance to set seed. By taking a proactive approach to weed management and embracing natural solutions, you'll create a garden that is not just free of chemicals, but teeming with life and vitality.

Patience and Persistence: Like a gardener tending to a delicate rose, managing pests and weeds without harmful chemicals requires patience and persistence. It may take time to see results, and there may be setbacks along the way, but with determination and dedication, you'll reap the rewards of a healthy and thriving garden. Stay vigilant, monitoring your garden regularly for signs of pests and weeds, and be prepared to take action when necessary. Remember that gardening is a journey, not a destination, and that every challenge is an opportunity to learn and grow. By embracing the process and staying true to your principles, you'll create a garden that is not just beautiful and bountiful, but in harmony with the natural world.

With each pest managed, each weed pulled, you're fostering a deeper sense of connection with the earth and all its inhabitants—a connection rooted in respect, compassion, and stewardship. So tend to your garden with love and care, and let it be a reflection of your commitment to living in harmony with nature.

Chapter 5 Attracting and Observing Pollinators

Providing Nesting Sites

Close your eyes and imagine a world alive with the sounds of nature—the rustle of leaves, the chirping of birds, the gentle buzz of bees. Now open your eyes and consider the creatures that call your garden home—the birds that sing from the treetops, the bees that buzz among the flowers, the butterflies that flit from bloom to bloom. How will you provide sanctuary for these precious creatures, offering them a place to rest, nest, and raise their young?

Shelter in the Branches: Imagine a cozy nest nestled among the branches of a tree—a safe haven where birds can raise their young away from prying eyes and predators. Trees and shrubs provide essential nesting sites for a wide variety of bird species, offering protection from the elements and a sturdy foundation for building their nests. Choose a mix of native trees and shrubs with dense foliage and sturdy branches, providing a range of nesting opportunities for birds of all shapes and sizes. By planting a diverse array of trees and shrubs, you'll create a welcoming habitat that attracts birds throughout the year, from nesting season in spring to migration in fall.

Burrows in the Earth: Picture a tunnel dug deep into the earth—a cozy burrow where rabbits, ground-dwelling birds, and other small mammals can take refuge from the elements and raise their young in safety. Burrows provide essential nesting sites for a variety of wildlife species, offering protection from predators and extreme weather conditions. Create habitat features like brush piles, rock piles, and log piles to provide shelter for ground-dwelling creatures, mimicking the natural habitats they depend on for survival. By incorporating these features into your garden landscape, you'll create a welcoming environment for wildlife of all kinds, fostering a sense of balance and harmony in the ecosystem.

Holes in the Walls: Imagine a cozy cavity tucked into the side of a building—a snug retreat where solitary bees, wasps, and other insects can build their nests and rear their offspring. Providing nesting sites for cavity-nesting insects is as simple as leaving dead trees standing, providing wooden nesting blocks, or installing purpose-built nesting boxes designed to attract specific species.

These artificial nesting sites mimic the natural cavities found in trees and are essential for supporting healthy populations of pollinators and other beneficial insects. By providing nesting sites for cavity-nesting insects, you'll create a garden that is not just beautiful and productive, but teeming with life and vitality.

Offering a Helping Hand: Like a welcoming host inviting guests into their home, providing nesting sites for wildlife is an act of kindness and compassion—a gesture of goodwill towards the creatures that share our world. Take the time to observe and understand the nesting habits and preferences of the wildlife species in your area, then take action to create habitat features that meet their needs. Whether it's planting trees and shrubs, leaving dead wood standing, or installing nesting boxes, every effort you make to provide nesting sites for wildlife contributes to the health and vitality of the ecosystem. By offering a helping hand to wildlife, you'll create a garden that is not just a sanctuary for creatures great and small, but a beacon of hope and resilience in an ever-changing world.

With each nesting site provided, each shelter offered, you're building a sanctuary—a place where wildlife can thrive and flourish, and where the natural world can be celebrated and cherished. So tend to your garden with love and care, and let it be a haven for creatures great and small.

Adding Water Sources

Close your eyes and imagine the soothing sound of water trickling over smooth stones—the cool touch of liquid refreshment on a hot summer's day. Now open your eyes and consider the creatures that share your garden—the bees seeking a drink, the birds splashing in a bath, the butterflies sipping from a puddle. How will you provide them with the life-giving gift of water, creating an oasis of hydration and vitality in your garden?

Pools of Reflection: Picture a still pool of water nestled among the greenery—a tranquil haven where birds can bathe and drink, where insects can dip their proboscis and quench their thirst. Adding a bird bath or shallow dish filled with clean, fresh water to your garden provides essential hydration for birds and other wildlife, especially during hot, dry weather. Choose a shallow dish with sloping sides to allow creatures to easily access the water and provide a few rocks or sticks for perches and landing spots. By offering a pool of reflection in your garden, you'll create a serene oasis where creatures can find respite and renewal amidst the hustle and bustle of the natural world.

Trickles of Life: Imagine a gentle stream winding its way through the landscape—the soft murmur of water cascading over rocks, the playful dance of light and shadow on the surface. Adding a water feature like a small fountain, pond, or waterfall to your garden not only provides a source of hydration for wildlife but also adds beauty, movement, and tranquility to the landscape. Choose a location that receives partial sunlight to prevent algae growth and ensure that the water remains clean and clear. By incorporating a trickle of life into your garden, you'll create a dynamic and inviting environment that attracts a wide variety of creatures, from birds and butterflies to frogs and dragonflies.

Dewdrops of Nectar: Picture a cluster of flowers glistening with dew—the sweet nectar of life beckoning to thirsty insects in need of refreshment. Adding nectar-rich flowers to your garden not only provides essential food for pollinators but also offers a source of hydration when water is scarce. Choose a mix of native flowers with tubular blossoms that hold water, like salvias, penstemons, and fuchsias, and plant them in clusters to create a buffet of nectar for bees, butterflies, and other insects. By offering dewdrops of nectar in your garden, you'll create a vibrant and inviting space where creatures can feast and flourish, nourished by the abundance of the natural world.

Offering a Helping Hand: Like a kind-hearted host offering a drink to a weary traveler, adding water sources to your garden is an act of compassion and generosity—an invitation to creatures great and small to quench their thirst and find solace in the midst of a busy world. Take the time to observe the needs and preferences of the wildlife in your area, then take action to provide water sources that meet their needs. Whether it's adding a bird bath, installing a water feature, or planting nectar-rich flowers, every effort you make to offer a helping hand to wildlife contributes to the health and vitality of the ecosystem. By providing water sources in your garden, you'll create a sanctuary—a place where creatures can find nourishment, renewal, and a sense of belonging in a world that can sometimes feel overwhelming.

With each drop of water offered, each ripple of life created, you're building an oasis—a sanctuary for creatures and souls alike, where the gift of water sustains and nourishes life in all its forms. So tend to your garden with love and care, and let it be a beacon of hope and renewal in an ever-changing world.

Tips For Observing And Identifying Pollinators In Your Garden

Close your eyes and imagine the gentle flutter of wings, the vibrant colors darting from bloom to bloom—the magical dance of pollinators in your garden. Now open your eyes and consider the wonders that await you as you embark on the journey of observing and identifying these essential creatures, each one a marvel of nature's design.

Patience and Presence: Like a quiet observer in a bustling market, patience and presence are key to observing pollinators in your garden. Take the time to sit quietly among the flowers, observing the comings and goings of bees, butterflies, and other pollinators as they go about their important work. Allow yourself to become fully present in the moment, tuning in to the sights, sounds, and sensations of the natural world around you. By cultivating a sense of calm and presence, you'll create an environment where pollinators feel safe and comfortable, allowing you to observe them up close without causing them undue stress or disturbance.

Close Encounters: Imagine yourself as a curious explorer, venturing into the heart of the garden to discover the secrets of its inhabitants. Get up close and personal with the flowers, observing the intricate details of their petals, the patterns of their veins, the subtle variations in color and scent. Take note of the pollinators that visit each flower, observing their size, shape, and behavior as they collect nectar and pollen. Use a magnifying glass or camera to capture close-up images of pollinators in action, allowing you to study their features and markings in greater detail. By getting close to the action, you'll gain a deeper appreciation for the beauty and complexity of the pollinator world, and develop a keen eye for identifying different species.

The Language of Pollinators: Like a skilled interpreter decoding a foreign language, learning to recognize the signs and signals of pollinators is essential to identifying them in your garden. Take note of the flight patterns, hovering behavior, and feeding preferences of different pollinator species, using these clues to help you narrow down their identities. Pay attention to the types of flowers they visit, the times of day they are most active, and the habitats they prefer, all of which can provide valuable insights into their identity and behavior. By learning the language of pollinators, you'll become fluent in the art of observation, and develop a deep understanding of the intricate web of life that unfolds in your garden.

Field Guides and Resources: Imagine yourself as a student in a vast library, surrounded by books and resources that hold the keys to unlocking the mysteries of the natural world. Arm yourself with field guides, identification charts, and online resources that can help you identify different pollinator species and learn more about their habits and habitats. Take advantage of citizen science programs like iNaturalist and Bumble Bee Watch, where you can upload photos of pollinators and receive help from experts in identifying them. Join local naturalist groups and gardening clubs, where you can connect with like-minded individuals who share your passion for pollinators and can offer guidance and support on your journey of discovery. By tapping into these valuable resources, you'll expand your knowledge and deepen your appreciation for the incredible diversity of pollinators that call your garden home.

Cultivating Curiosity: Like a child exploring a new playground, cultivating curiosity is essential to unlocking the wonders of the pollinator world. Approach each observation with a sense of wonder and awe, allowing yourself to be captivated by the beauty and intricacy of the creatures you encounter. Ask questions, seek answers, and never stop learning about the fascinating world of pollinators that surrounds you. By cultivating curiosity, you'll open yourself up to endless opportunities for discovery and delight, and forge a deeper connection with the natural world that sustains and inspires us all.

With each observation you make, each pollinator you identify, you're embarking on a journey of discovery—a journey that holds the promise of endless wonder and fascination. So step into the garden with an open heart and a curious mind, and let the dance of pollinators be your guide to the beauty and abundance of the natural world.

Chapter 6 Seasonal Care and Year-Round Interest

Planning For Continuous Bloom Throughout The Seasons

Close your eyes and envision a garden that never sleeps—a tapestry of color and fragrance that unfolds like a symphony, each season bringing its own melody to the chorus of life. Now open your eyes and consider the magic that awaits you as you embark on the journey of planning for continuous bloom throughout the seasons, each flower a testament to the timeless rhythm of nature's song.

Embracing the Cycle: Like a dancer moving gracefully through the steps of a waltz, planning for continuous bloom throughout the seasons requires an understanding and appreciation of the natural cycles that govern the garden. Embrace the ebb and flow of the seasons, observing the changing patterns of light and temperature, and the shifting rhythms of growth and dormancy. Choose plants that bloom at different times of the year, from early spring bulbs to late summer perennials, ensuring that your garden is alive with color and fragrance no matter the season. By embracing the cycle of life in your garden, you'll create a space that is in harmony with the natural world, and that offers something new and beautiful to discover with each passing month.

Creating a Tapestry of Color: Imagine yourself as an artist, painting with a palette of flowers in every hue and shade imaginable—reds and yellows, blues and purples, whites and pinks. Choose a diverse mix of annuals, perennials, bulbs, and shrubs that bloom at different times throughout the year, and that offer a range of colors, shapes, and textures to delight the senses. Plant them in drifts and clusters, mixing and mingling them together to create a tapestry of color that evolves and changes with the seasons. By creating a garden that is alive with color throughout the year, you'll transform your outdoor space into a living work of art—one that brings joy and inspiration to all who behold it.

Nurturing the Nectar: Like a host preparing a feast for guests, planning for continuous bloom throughout the seasons requires careful attention to the needs of pollinators and other wildlife that rely on your garden for housing and nourishment. Choose plants that offer nectar and pollen for bees, butterflies, and other pollinators throughout the year, ensuring that there is always something in bloom to sustain them. Include a mix of native and non-native species, as well as plants with different flower shapes and sizes, to attract a diverse array of pollinators to your garden. By nurturing the nectar in your garden, you'll create a haven for wildlife—a place where creatures great and small can find sustenance and solace in a world that is increasingly fragmented and diminished.

__Cultivating Connection:__ Like a gardener tending to a cherished friend, planning for continuous bloom throughout the seasons is an act of love and devotion—a commitment to nurturing the beauty and abundance of the natural world. Take the time to observe and appreciate the subtle changes that occur in your garden throughout the year, from the first snowdrops of spring to the last asters of autumn. Share your garden with others, inviting friends and family to join you in the joy of discovery and exploration. By cultivating connection with your garden and with the world around you, you'll deepen your appreciation for the wonders of nature and forge a deeper bond with the earth and all its inhabitants.

With each seed you sow, each flower that blooms, you're sowing the seeds of time—a garden that is not just beautiful and bountiful, but alive with the magic of the changing seasons. So plan for continuous bloom with love and care, and let your garden be a sanctuary—a place of beauty, wonder, and everlasting joy.

Winterizing Your Garden

Close your eyes and imagine the gentle kiss of frost on the tips of leaves—the quiet stillness of a garden blanketed in snow, the promise of renewal hidden beneath the surface. Now open your eyes and consider the tasks that lie ahead as you prepare your garden for the harsh embrace of winter, each one a gesture of care and protection for the plants that have brought you so much joy and beauty throughout the year.

Tending to Tender Plants: Like a parent tucking their child into bed on a cold winter's night, tending to tender plants is an act of love and protection—a commitment to nurturing their delicate spirits through the harshest of seasons. Before the first frost arrives, take the time to tenderly dig up any tender bulbs or plants that won't survive the winter outdoors. Wrap their roots in moist paper towels or newspaper, place them in a cardboard box filled with peat moss or vermiculite, and store them in a cool, dark place until spring. By giving tender plants a cozy place to rest during the winter months, you'll ensure that they emerge from their slumber refreshed and ready to bloom again in the spring.

Mulching for Warmth: Imagine a cozy blanket spread over the earth—a layer of mulch that protects the soil from the chill of winter and provides a warm haven for dormant plants and beneficial organisms. Before the ground freezes solid, spread a thick layer of organic mulch, such as straw, shredded leaves, or wood chips, over your garden beds and around the base of trees and shrubs. This will help insulate the soil, regulate temperature fluctuations, and prevent frost heaving, where freezing and thawing cycles can push plants out of the ground. By mulching your garden for warmth, you'll create a cozy refuge for plants and soil life alike, ensuring that they weather the winter months with grace and resilience.

Pruning with Care: Like a skilled barber shaping a hedge, pruning with care is an art form—a delicate balance of shaping and sculpting, of removing the old to make way for the new. Before winter sets in, take the time to prune back any dead, diseased, or damaged branches from trees, shrubs, and perennials. This will not only improve the overall health and appearance of your plants but also reduce the risk of winter damage from heavy snow and ice. Use sharp, clean pruners to make clean cuts just above a healthy bud or branch junction, and avoid removing more than one-third of the plant's total growth in a single pruning session. By pruning with care, you'll create a garden that is not just beautiful, but healthy and resilient in the face of winter's challenges.

Sheltering Wildlife: Imagine yourself as a compassionate host, welcoming guests into your home and offering them a warm place to rest and recharge during the long winter months. Create habitat features like brush piles, rock piles, and birdhouses to provide shelter for birds, insects, and other wildlife that depend on your garden for food and shelter. Leave seed heads and dried flower stalks standing in the garden to provide food for birds and other creatures, and consider leaving a portion of your garden beds unplanted to provide habitat for overwintering insects and other beneficial organisms. By sheltering wildlife in your garden, you'll create a sanctuary—a place where creatures great and small can find refuge and solace in a world that can sometimes feel cold and inhospitable.

Cultivating Gratitude: Like a gardener tending to their beloved plants, winterizing your garden is an act of gratitude—an acknowledgment of the beauty and abundance that the natural world provides, even in the darkest of times. Take a moment to pause and reflect on the blessings that your garden has brought you throughout the year—the joy of seeing a flower bloom, the satisfaction of harvesting a ripe tomato, the wonder of witnessing the dance of pollinators in the summer sun. Give thanks for the abundance of life that surrounds you, and for the opportunity to steward the land with care and reverence. By cultivating gratitude in your garden, you'll deepen your connection

to the earth and all its inhabitants, and find solace and strength in the knowledge that spring will come again, bringing with it the promise of new life and growth.

With each task completed, each plant tucked in for the winter, you're nurturing the beauty and resilience of your garden—a sanctuary that will weather the storms of winter and emerge renewed and revitalized in the spring. So winterize your garden with love and care, and let it be a testament to the power of nature to heal, to nourish, and to inspire.

Chapter 7 Troubleshooting Common Issues

Dealing With Pests And Diseases

Close your eyes and envision the tender leaves of your plants, the vibrant blooms reaching for the sun—the delicate balance of life teeming in your garden. Now, open your eyes and confront the challenges that arise when pests and diseases threaten this delicate harmony, each one a reminder of the fragility and resilience of the natural world.

Vigilance and Observation: Like a watchful guardian, vigilance and observation are your greatest tools in the battle against pests and diseases. Take the time to inspect your plants regularly, noting any changes in their appearance or behavior—yellowing leaves, chewed edges, wilting stems. Look for signs of pests like aphids, caterpillars, and beetles, as well as symptoms of diseases like powdery mildew, leaf spot, and blight. By staying vigilant and observant, you'll catch problems early and be better equipped to take action before they escalate.

Cultivating Resilience: Imagine yourself as a healer, tending to the wounds of your plants with care and compassion. Cultivating resilience in your garden is essential to preventing and managing pests and diseases. Start by choosing healthy, disease-resistant plants and providing them with the proper growing conditions—plenty of sunlight, well-drained soil, and adequate moisture. Avoid overcrowding plants, which can create conditions favorable to pests and diseases, and rotate crops each year to break up pest and disease cycles. By cultivating resilience in your garden, you'll create an environment where plants can thrive and resist the onslaught of pests and diseases.

Natural Solutions: Like a master chef crafting a gourmet meal, natural solutions offer a menu of options for dealing with pests and diseases in your garden. Consider using biological controls like beneficial insects, nematodes, and predatory mites to target specific pests without harming beneficial organisms. Use organic pesticides and fungicides made from natural ingredients like neem oil, garlic, and potassium bicarbonate to manage pest and disease outbreaks without resorting to harsh chemicals. And don't forget the power of cultural practices like pruning, sanitation, and crop rotation to prevent and control pests and diseases in your garden. By embracing natural solutions, you'll create a safer, healthier environment for yourself, your plants, and all the creatures that call your garden home.

Compassion and Understanding: Like a compassionate friend offering a listening ear, dealing with pests and diseases in your garden requires empathy and understanding. Remember that pests and diseases are not malicious invaders, but simply creatures trying to survive in a complex and interconnected ecosystem. Take the time to learn about the life cycles and habits of common pests and diseases in your area, and consider their needs and motivations when devising control strategies. Seek out alternative solutions whenever possible, and avoid resorting to chemical interventions that can harm beneficial organisms and disrupt the delicate balance of your garden. By approaching pest and disease management with compassion and understanding, you'll create a more harmonious and sustainable environment for all living things.

Persistence and Adaptation: Like a gardener weathering the storms of life, persistence and adaptation are essential qualities in the face of pest and disease challenges. Be prepared to try different approaches and techniques until you find what works best for your garden, and don't be discouraged by setbacks or failures along the way. Stay flexible and open-minded, willing to adapt your strategies as needed to meet the ever-changing needs of your garden and the creatures that inhabit it. By persisting and adapting in the face of adversity, you'll cultivate a sense of resilience and empowerment that will serve you well in all areas of your life.

With each pest managed, each disease controlled, you're nurturing the health and vitality of your garden—a sanctuary of beauty and abundance in an ever-changing world. So tend to your garden with love and care, and let it be a testament to the power of human ingenuity and compassion to overcome even the greatest challenges.

Addressing Poor Pollinator Activity

Close your eyes and imagine the gentle hum of bees buzzing among the flowers—the flutter of butterflies dancing on the breeze, the delicate touch of a pollinator's wings against your skin. Now, open your eyes and confront the challenge of addressing poor pollinator activity in your garden, each moment an opportunity to reconnect with the rhythm of nature and restore balance to the world around you.

Observation and Reflection: Like a wise sage gazing into a crystal ball, observation and reflection are your guides on the journey to understanding and addressing poor pollinator activity. Take the time to sit quietly in your garden, observing the comings and goings of pollinators—or the lack thereof. Notice any changes in pollinator behavior or abundance, and consider possible factors that may be contributing to the decline in activity. Are there fewer flowers blooming than usual? Has there been a change in weather patterns or habitat conditions? By reflecting on these questions, you'll gain valuable insights into the underlying causes of poor pollinator activity and be better equipped to take action.

Creating Habitat and Resources: Imagine yourself as a guardian of the land, tasked with providing sanctuary and sustenance for all who dwell within your garden. Creating habitat and resources for pollinators is essential to restoring balance and vitality to your garden ecosystem. Start by planting a diverse array of flowers that bloom throughout the growing season, providing nectar and pollen for bees, butterflies, and other pollinators. Choose native plants whenever possible, as they are best adapted to the local climate and provide the greatest benefit to native pollinators. Incorporate habitat features like bee hotels, butterfly houses, and water sources to provide shelter, nesting sites, and hydration for pollinators. By creating a welcoming environment for pollinators, you'll encourage them to return to your garden year after year, ensuring a healthy and vibrant ecosystem for generations to come.

Avoiding Harmful Practices: Like a steward of the land, avoiding harmful practices is essential to protecting the delicate balance of your garden ecosystem. Avoid using pesticides, herbicides, and other chemical treatments that can harm pollinators and disrupt the natural harmony of your garden. Instead, opt for organic and sustainable gardening practices that support the health and well-being of all living things. Practice integrated pest management (IPM) techniques to manage pest populations without resorting to harmful chemicals, and use cultural practices like crop rotation, companion planting, and soil amendment to promote soil health and reduce the risk of disease. By avoiding harmful practices and embracing a holistic approach to gardening, you'll create a garden that is not just beautiful, but resilient and sustainable in the face of environmental challenges.

Cultivating Connection: Like a bridge connecting two worlds, cultivating connection is essential to restoring harmony and balance to your garden ecosystem. Reach out to local community groups, gardening clubs, and conservation organizations to learn more about pollinators and how you can support their conservation efforts. Share your knowledge and experiences with others, inspiring them to take action in their own gardens and communities. By cultivating connection with others who share your passion for pollinators, you'll amplify your impact and create a ripple effect of positive change that extends far beyond the borders of your garden.

Embracing Patience and Hope: Like a gardener tending to a seedling, embracing patience and hope is essential to restoring balance and vitality to your garden ecosystem. Trust in the inherent resilience of nature, and have faith that with time and care, pollinator activity will return to your garden once again. Be patient with yourself and with the natural world, knowing that change takes time and that every small action you take makes a difference. By embracing patience and hope, you'll cultivate a sense of optimism and possibility that will carry you through even the darkest of times.

With each flower planted, each habitat created, you're sowing the seeds of hope and renewal—a garden that is not just beautiful, but alive with the buzz of pollinators and the promise of a brighter future. So tend to your garden with love and care, and let it be a beacon of hope and inspiration in a world that is hungry for connection and renewal.

Chapter 8 Community And Environmental Impact

Engaging With Local Organizations And Communities

Close your eyes and imagine the warmth of a handshake, the laughter shared over a cup of tea—the sense of belonging that comes from connecting with others who share your passion and purpose. Now, open your eyes and consider the power of engaging with local organizations and communities, each interaction an opportunity to build bridges, forge friendships, and make a difference in the world around you.

Finding Common Ground: Like a traveler in a foreign land, finding common ground is the first step on the journey of engagement. Reach out to local organizations and communities that share your interest in gardening, conservation, or environmental stewardship, and explore opportunities to connect and collaborate on shared goals and projects. Attend community events, workshops, and meetings to meet like-minded individuals and learn more about the issues and challenges facing your local area. By finding common ground with others, you'll lay the foundation for meaningful connections and partnerships that can make a real difference in your community.

Sharing Knowledge and Resources: Imagine yourself as a teacher, sharing your wisdom and expertise with others who are eager to learn and grow. Engaging with local organizations and communities is an opportunity to share your knowledge and resources with others, helping to empower them to take action in their own lives and communities. Offer to lead workshops, give presentations, or host garden tours to share your passion for gardening and conservation with others. Share your favorite tips and techniques for creating pollinator-friendly gardens, reducing waste, conserving water, and more. By sharing your knowledge and resources with others, you'll inspire and empower them to make positive changes in their own lives and communities.

Building Relationships: Like a gardener tending to their plants, building relationships takes time, patience, and care. Take the time to get to know the people in your local organizations and communities, listening to their stories, learning about their passions and concerns, and finding ways to support and uplift them in their efforts. Offer a helping hand to those in need, whether it's volunteering at a community garden, participating in a neighborhood cleanup, or lending a sympathetic ear to someone who's struggling. By building relationships with others, you'll create a sense of belonging and camaraderie that strengthens the bonds of community and fosters a spirit of cooperation and mutual support.

Fostering Collaboration: Like a conductor leading an orchestra, fostering collaboration is about bringing together diverse voices and talents to create something beautiful and harmonious. Engage with local organizations and communities to identify shared goals and priorities, and explore opportunities to collaborate on projects and initiatives that benefit the greater good. Whether it's organizing a community garden project, launching a neighborhood tree planting campaign, or advocating for policies that protect and preserve the environment, working together with others allows you to amplify your impact and achieve greater success than you could alone. By fostering collaboration with others, you'll create a sense of unity and purpose that transcends individual differences and brings people together in service of a common cause.

Cultivating Compassion: Like a gardener nurturing a delicate seedling, cultivating compassion is about caring for others with kindness, empathy, and understanding. Engage with local organizations and communities with an open heart and a spirit of compassion, recognizing the humanity and dignity of each individual you encounter. Listen with empathy to the stories of those who are struggling or marginalized, and seek to understand the challenges they face. Offer your support and solidarity to those in need, whether it's through acts of kindness, advocacy, or simply being a compassionate presence in their lives. By cultivating compassion in your interactions with others, you'll create a culture of caring and empathy that uplifts and sustains the human spirit, fostering a sense of connection and belonging for all.

With each connection made, each relationship built, you're sowing the seeds of community—a garden of hearts and hands united in service of a common cause. So engage with local organizations and communities with love and care, and let your actions be a testament to the power of human connection to create positive change in the world.

Promoting Awareness & Education About Pollinator Conservation

Close your eyes and imagine the delicate flutter of wings, the vibrant hues of petals—the intricate dance of pollinators and flowers, a symphony of life that sustains us all. Now, open your eyes and consider the vital role of promoting awareness and education about pollinator conservation, each conversation an opportunity to shine a light on the importance of protecting these essential creatures and the ecosystems they inhabit.

Cultivating Curiosity: Like a beacon in the night, promoting awareness and education about pollinator conservation is about sparking curiosity and wonder in the hearts and minds of others. Share stories and anecdotes about the fascinating lives of pollinators, from the incredible journeys of migratory butterflies to the intricate social structures of honeybee colonies. Invite others to join you in the garden, where they can witness firsthand the beauty and diversity of pollinators in action. Encourage questions and curiosity, inviting others to explore and discover the wonders of the natural world for themselves. By cultivating curiosity, you'll inspire others to take an active interest in pollinator conservation and become stewards of the earth in their own right.

Raising Awareness: Like a lighthouse guiding ships safely to shore, raising awareness about pollinator conservation is about shining a light on the importance of protecting these vital creatures and the habitats they depend on. Take every opportunity to raise awareness about the threats facing pollinators, from habitat loss and pesticide exposure to climate change and invasive species. Share articles, videos, and other educational resources that highlight the importance of pollinators to our food supply, biodiversity, and overall well-being. Participate in community events, workshops, and outreach programs that focus on pollinator conservation, reaching out to people of all ages and backgrounds to spread the message far and wide. By raising awareness about pollinator conservation, you'll help others understand the urgency of the situation and inspire them to take action to protect these essential creatures.

Empowering Action: Like a torch passed from hand to hand, empowering action is about giving others the tools and resources they need to make a positive difference in the world. Offer practical tips and advice for creating pollinator-friendly habitats in gardens, parks, and other green spaces, from planting native flowers and avoiding pesticides to providing nesting sites and water sources for pollinators. Organize volunteer opportunities and community projects that focus on pollinator conservation, giving people a chance to roll up their sleeves and get involved in hands-on conservation efforts. Advocate for policies and practices that support pollinator conservation at the local, state, and national levels, mobilizing others to join you in speaking out for the protection of pollinators and their habitats. By empowering action, you'll transform awareness into tangible change, creating a ripple effect of positive impact that extends far beyond your own efforts.

Fostering Connection: Like a bridge spanning a river, fostering connection is about building relationships and creating a sense of belonging among all who share a passion for pollinator conservation. Connect with local organizations, schools, businesses, and government agencies that are working to protect pollinators, forging partnerships and collaborations that amplify your collective impact. Reach out to people from diverse backgrounds and communities, inviting them to join you in the journey of pollinator conservation and offering support and encouragement along the way. Create opportunities for people to come together and share their experiences, ideas, and expertise, fostering a sense of community and camaraderie that strengthens the bonds of solidarity and collective action. By fostering connection, you'll create a network of allies and advocates who are united in their commitment to pollinator conservation and who support one another in their shared mission.

Cultivating Hope: Like a seed planted in fertile soil, cultivating hope is about nurturing the belief that positive change is possible, even in the face of daunting challenges. Share success stories and examples of communities coming together to protect pollinators and restore habitat, inspiring others to believe in the power of collective action and resilience. Highlight the efforts of individuals, organizations, and governments around the world that are making a difference in the fight to save pollinators, celebrating their achievements and recognizing the impact of their work. Offer words of encouragement and support to those who may feel overwhelmed or discouraged by the magnitude of the task ahead, reminding them that every small action they take makes a difference and that together, we can create a brighter future for pollinators and all living things. By cultivating hope, you'll instill a sense of optimism and determination in others, fueling their passion and commitment to pollinator conservation and inspiring them to keep moving forward, one step at a time.

With each conversation had, each awareness raised, you're shining a light on the path to pollinator preservation—a journey of discovery, connection, and collective action that holds the promise of a better world for all. So let your voice be heard, your actions be felt, and your heart be open to the possibility of positive change. Together, we can protect pollinators and the precious ecosystems they inhabit, ensuring a future where flowers bloom, fruits ripen, and life flourishes in all its abundance and diversity.

15 Days Gardening Tracker

GARDENING PLANNER

Dates _______________

	MORNING	AFTERNOON	EVENING
MON			
TUE			
WED			
THU			
FRI			
SAT			
SUN			

NOTE:
_______________ _______________ _______________
_______________ _______________ _______________
_______________ _______________ _______________
_______________ _______________ _______________
_______________ _______________ _______________

GARDENING PLANNER

Dates ___________

	MORNING	AFTERNOON	EVENING
MON			
TUE			
WED			
THU			
FRI			
SAT			
SUN			

NOTE:

GARDENING PLANNER

Dates ___________

	MORNING	AFTERNOON	EVENING
MON			
TUE			
WED			
THU			
FRI			
SAT			
SUN			

NOTE:

GARDENING PLANNER

Dates ______________________

	MORNING	AFTERNOON	EVENING
MON			
TUE			
WED			
THU			
FRI			
SAT			
SUN			

NOTE:

GARDENING PLANNER

Dates
____

	MORNING	AFTERNOON	EVENING
MON			
TUE			
WED			
THU			
FRI			
SAT			
SUN			

NOTE:

GARDENING PLANNER

Dates

	MORNING	AFTERNOON	EVENING
MON			
TUE			
WED			
THU			
FRI			
SAT			
SUN			

NOTE:

GARDENING PLANNER

Dates ___________________

	MORNING	AFTERNOON	EVENING
MON			
TUE			
WED			
THU			
FRI			
SAT			
SUN			

NOTE:

GARDENING PLANNER

Dates
____

	MORNING	AFTERNOON	EVENING
MON			
TUE			
WED			
THU			
FRI			
SAT			
SUN			

NOTE:
_______________ _______________ _______________
_______________ _______________ _______________
_______________ _______________ _______________
_______________ _______________ _______________
_______________ _______________ _______________

GARDENING PLANNER

Dates ____________________

	MORNING	AFTERNOON	EVENING
MON			
TUE			
WED			
THU			
FRI			
SAT			
SUN			

NOTE:

GARDENING PLANNER

Dates
____

	MORNING	AFTERNOON	EVENING
MON			
TUE			
WED			
THU			
FRI			
SAT			
SUN			

NOTE:

GARDENING PLANNER

Dates
____

	MORNING	AFTERNOON	EVENING
MON			
TUE			
WED			
THU			
FRI			
SAT			
SUN			

NOTE:

_______________ _______________ _______________
_______________ _______________ _______________
_______________ _______________ _______________
_______________ _______________ _______________
_______________ _______________ _______________
_______________ _______________ _______________

GARDENING PLANNER

Dates

____

	MORNING	AFTERNOON	EVENING
MON			
TUE			
WED			
THU			
FRI			
SAT			
SUN			

NOTE:

GARDENING PLANNER

Dates ____________________

	MORNING	AFTERNOON	EVENING
MON			
TUE			
WED			
THU			
FRI			
SAT			
SUN			

NOTE:

GARDENING PLANNER

Dates ______________

	MORNING	AFTERNOON	EVENING
MON			
TUE			
WED			
THU			
FRI			
SAT			
SUN			

NOTE:
________________ ________________ ________________
________________ ________________ ________________
________________ ________________ ________________
________________ ________________ ________________
________________ ________________ ________________

GARDENING PLANNER

Dates ______________________

	MORNING	AFTERNOON	EVENING
MON			
TUE			
WED			
THU			
FRI			
SAT			
SUN			

NOTE:

______________ ______________ ______________
______________ ______________ ______________
______________ ______________ ______________
______________ ______________ ______________
______________ ______________ ______________
______________ ______________ ______________